W9-AEY-811

Guglielmo
MARCONI

Dr. Mike Goldsmith

RAINTREE
Steck-Vaughn
PUBLISHERS

A Harcourt Company

Austin   New York
www.raintreesteckvaughn.com

Published by Raintree Steck-Vaughn Publishers, an imprint of Steck-Vaughn Company

Library of Congress Cataloging-in-Publication

Goldsmith, Mike, Dr.
    Guglielmo Marconi/Mike Goldsmith.
       p.cm.—(scientists who made history)
    Summary: Describes the life and work of the Italian inventor Marconi, who was a pioneer in the development of the radio.
    Includes bibliographical references and index.
    ISBN 0-7398-5227-2
    1. Marconi, Guglielmo, marchese, 1874-1937—Juvenile literature. 2. Inventors—Italy—Biography—Juvenile literature. 3. Radio—History—Juvenile literature. [1. Marconi, Guglielmo, marchese, 1874-1937. 2. Inventors. 3. Radio—History.] I. Title. II. Series.

TK5739.M3 G65 2002
621.384'092—dc21   2002016374

Printed in Hong Kong. Bound in the United States.

1 2 3 4 5 6 7 8 9 0 LB 07 06 05 04 03 02

Picture Acknowledgments: Camera Press 12; Sue Cunningham 41l; Eye Ubiquitious 43; Guildhall Art Gallery, Corporation of London/Bridgeman Art Library 15; Hodder Wayland 10, 11; Mary Evans cover/title page, 6, 16, 22, 28, 29t, 31, 36; Marconi PLC 1, 8, 17, 18, 19, 20, 24l, 24r, 25, 26, 27t, 29b, 30t, 30b, 32, 33t, 34, 37t, 37b, 38, 40, 41l; Zul Mukhida 42t; Robert Opie 35b; Popperfoto 27b, 35t; Private Collection/Bridgeman Art Library 9; Science Photo Library 7, 21, 33b, 42b.

Contents

A Signal Through the Storm

GUGLIELMO MARCONI CROUCHED over the jumble of apparatus, frowning in concentration. Around him a gale howled and moaned, battering the rocky coastline of Newfoundland, Canada. But Guglielmo wasn't listening to the wind. He was concentrating on the hiss from the tiny loudspeaker in his ear. A wire led from the loudspeaker to the equipment in front of him, and another wire led up into the air to where a kite curved and swooped through the stormy sky. Guglielmo knew that on the other side of the ocean in Cornwall, England, his assistant was tapping out a message over and over again. Many people thought no signal could travel so far—surely it would be absorbed by the Earth?

This wasn't Guglielmo's first attempt. Vast aerials had been erected on both sides of the Atlantic but they'd all been torn down by autumn gales. Yesterday he and his team had tried to mount an aerial on a balloon, but that too had been ripped

BELOW: *Guglielmo Marconi, with the apparatus he used to detect the first radio message sent across the Atlantic Ocean in 1901.*

away by the wind. So today—December 12, 1901—they were using kites. The first had already been lost and now the storm was closing in again. Would this be another failure?

Contact

Then suddenly, through the roar of the gale and the hiss of static, Guglielmo heard it, briefly but unmistakably—the triple beep of the signal, repeated over and over again. The gale worsened and the signal was lost, but it didn't matter now. He'd done it. He'd heard a radio message from across the Atlantic.

RIGHT: *There is a whole range of electromagnetic waves of different lengths, which together form the electromagnetic spectrum.*

RADIO WAVES

The range of colors from violet through blue, green, yellow, and orange to red is called the visible spectrum. But there are other invisible "colors" outside this range. Beyond red is infrared, and beyond that are radio waves.

Like light, radio waves are a form of energy that travels through space at incredible speed, in the form of a wave (see right). The only difference between light and radio waves is the length of the waves: light waves are much less than a thousandth of an inch long, while radio waves range from a fraction of an inch to a few miles in length.

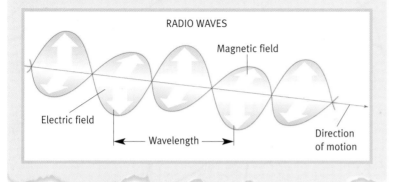

RADIO WAVES

Magnetic field

Electric field

← Wavelength →

Direction of motion

ABOVE: *Here you see both the electric and magnetic parts of the radio wave.*

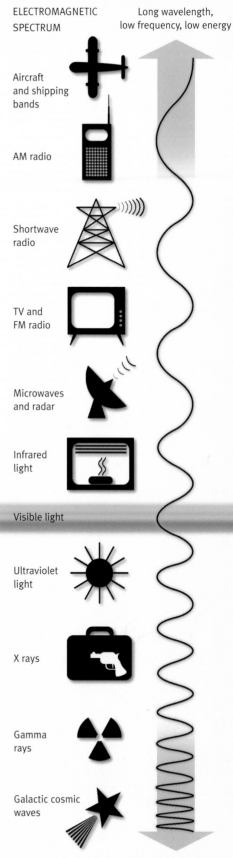

ELECTROMAGNETIC SPECTRUM

Long wavelength, low frequency, low energy

Aircraft and shipping bands

AM radio

Shortwave radio

TV and FM radio

Microwaves and radar

Infrared light

Visible light

Ultraviolet light

X rays

Gamma rays

Galactic cosmic waves

Short wavelength, high frequency, high energy

Before Radio

UNTIL MARCONI'S breakthrough with wireless (as radio was then called), there was a big difference between communication on land and over the sea. On land, telegraph wires had been laid between many towns and cities, and messages were sent along them. These messages were mostly in the form of Morse code: patterns of short and long signals that represented the letters of the alphabet.

BELOW: *The transatlantic telegraph cable being laid from the* **Great Eastern** *steamship.*

Before 1866 the only way to communicate across the Atlantic Ocean was by ship, but finally, after years of work and many failures, a working telegraph cable was laid across the ocean floor. Europe and America were linked at last, and messages could be exchanged in minutes instead of weeks.

However, there were still many difficulties. Although several other transatlantic cables soon joined the first one, they were slow, very expensive, and could only send a few messages at a time. And there were no such links across the world's other oceans.

Another problem was that there was no way of sending telegraph messages to or from ships. If a ship was in danger, it could signal for help only by sending up flares, sounding cannons, or raising flags. So if there was no other ship within a few miles, there was little hope of rescue.

Invisible Rays

There did seem to be a possible solution to these problems. In 1873, James Clerk-Maxwell had predicted the existence of an undiscovered form of radiation, similar to light but invisible. Then in 1887, Heinrich Hertz not only proved that these waves existed, but managed to use them to send a signal a few yards. Could these waves be used to transmit messages over long distances? It seemed possible, but despite efforts by many scientists their range remained hopelessly limited.

BELOW: *James Clerk-Maxwell, the scientist who predicted the existence of radio waves in 1873.*

Early Years

GUGLIELMO MARCONI, the man who changed the face of communication forever, was born into a wealthy family in Bologna, Italy, in 1874. His father was Italian and his mother Irish. Marconi was always close to his mother and in his early years he had a good relationship with his father, too. They both loved the sea, and his father wanted him to become a naval officer.

The problems started when Marconi began to do badly at school. He didn't have the patience for things that bored him, and the only subject he liked was science. Unfortunately, science was not taught much at school, so Marconi educated himself, reading about famous scientists, doing experiments, and building scientific apparatus.

BELOW: *Guglielmo, age 6 (left), with his mother Annie and his brother Alfonso.*

The Young Scientist

His mother encouraged his curiosity, but his father could see no point in his activities. When Marconi accidentally broke a whole set of family china while trying an electrical demonstration, his father became determined to stop any further experiments. He was even less pleased when Marconi failed to gain entrance to the Naval Academy and had to make do with the Leghorn Technical Institute instead. In fact, the Institute was ideal for Marconi, because he could study science there.

Marconi's favorite area of science was electricity, and he imitated some of the experiments carried out by the American scientist Benjamin Franklin. It seemed that he could hope for a scientific career, despite

ABOVE: *The American scientist Benjamin Franklin, studying lightning in 1752. He showed that lightning is a form of electricity.*

his father, until he failed the entrance examinations for Bologna University. However, by an amazing piece of luck, Professor Augusto Righi, an eminent scientist who specialized in electricity, lived nearby and agreed to allow Marconi to use both his laboratory and the university library. If he could deal with his father's objections, perhaps Marconi could become a scientist after all.

IN THEIR OWN WORDS

"His father…imagined that he was just wasting his time. He would stomp irritably about the house, remarking sarcastically that it would be nice if Guglielmo would occasionally honor them by his presence."

NORMAN WYMER, IN HIS BOOK ABOUT MARCONI, *FROM MARCONI TO TELSTAR* (LONGMAN, 1966).

THE LEGACY OF HERTZ

Although Righi greatly helped Marconi by giving him access to the resources he needed, he was less encouraging when Marconi explained his plan to achieve long-distance radio communication. Righi told him flatly that he had no hope of success. The only person who really believed in him was his mother. Together, they set up a laboratory in the attic, well out of his father's way. Marconi worked there through the late autumn of 1894, often missing sleep and meals in his determination to make his radio system work.

Marconi's First Radio

Marconi built a radio system similar to the one Hertz had made (see page 7), with some improvements based on Righi's work. In particular, Hertz's primitive spark-gap receiver was replaced with a more sensitive device called a coherer (see right), which had been invented by French scientist Edouard Branley in 1892.

At this stage, Marconi's grasp of the physics behind radio communication was very limited.

LEFT: *Heinrich Hertz, the German scientist who proved in 1887 that radio waves exist.*

However, he faithfully followed descriptions given in scientific papers until, toward the end of the year, he was able to do more or less what Hertz had done thirteen years before: ring a bell at one end of his laboratory by sending a radio signal from the other. As far as Righi and the textbooks were concerned, this was the end of the story. But Marconi was sure that it was only the beginning.

IN THEIR OWN WORDS

"It seemed to me that if the radiation could be increased, developed, and controlled, it would be possible to signal across space for considerable distances. My chief trouble was that the idea was so elementary, so simple in logic, that it seemed difficult to believe no one else had thought of putting it into practice. I argued, there must be more mature scientists who had followed the same line of thought and arrived at similar conclusions. From the first, the idea was so real to me that I did not realize that to others the theory might appear quite fantastic."

MARCONI

MARCONI'S WIRELESS

In Marconi's first experiments, his radio transmitter consisted of an electrical device that could produce sparks. The sparks generated bursts of radio waves that were reflected by a curved metal plate to the receiver a few yards away. The receiver was more sophisticated than the one Hertz had used. The radio waves caused iron filings in the coherer to stick together (or "cohere") and conduct electricity from a battery. The electricity then flowed through an electrical buzzer(see page 12).

RIGHT: *A primitive coherer of the type Marconi first used.*

BEYOND THE HORIZON

Marconi was a highly organized, methodical, and patient person. These qualities were essential to his success. The best scientists in the world had no idea how to increase the range of radio signals, and Marconi was nowhere near the best. All he could do was experiment, tirelessly modifying his equipment in every possible way and testing the effect on its range.

As the months passed and the summer of 1895 began, Marconi slowly progressed. He improved the coherer by changing the type of filings it contained, by altering the shape of the electrical contacts, and finally by removing the air from it. Then he modified the transmitter, adding plates to the spark-producer.

BELOW: *Marconi, experimenting with an early version of his radio communication system. He is tapping out a message in Morse code, which is being picked up by the receiver in the distance. The two metal plates are the aerials.*

THE COHERER

The coherer was the part of early radio receivers that detected the presence of a radio signal. Because the signal is electromagnetic, it causes the metal filings to stick together so that the coherer conducts electricity. The electricity is then used to ring a bell or buzzer.

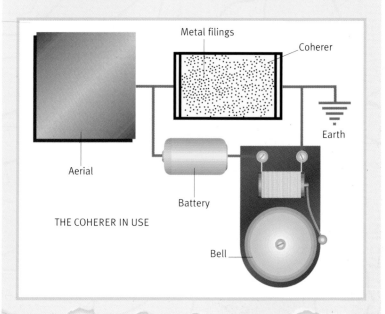

THE COHERER IN USE

Over the months, the range increased to the far end of the attic, to the floor below, and to the floor below that until, finally, he could send a signal that would make a buzzer sound outside on the terrace.

Soon, through a patient, methodical process of trial and error, Marconi made a real breakthrough. He connected one plate of the spark-gap to a sheet of metal that was raised in the air and the other plate to another sheet that rested on the ground. He attached similar metal sheets to the receiver, and was overjoyed to find that the range of the signals increased from a few yards to almost a mile. He would soon call the ground sheet the "earth" and the upper sheet the "aerial."

Marconi quickly discovered that he achieved even better results by making his aerials out of copper wire instead of metal sheets and by burying the "earth" in the ground. But he did not stop there. Helped by friends and farm workers, he sent signals farther and farther afield. To his surprise, he found that they could be detected even when there was a hill in the way! He could only assume the waves passed right through it.

IN THEIR OWN WORDS

"…the waves were going through or over the hill. It is my belief that they went through, but I do not wish to state it as a fact. I am not certain."

MARCONI IN 1897.

THE IONOSPHERE

The reason Marconi was able to receive radio signals even when there was a hill between receiver and transmitter was not that the waves went through the earth. High in the atmosphere there is a region called the ionosphere that contains charged particles. The ionosphere reflects some radio waves like a mirror reflects light and makes long-range radio communication possible.

LEFT: *The Villa Griffone, Marconi's childhood home near Bologna, where his early experiments took place.*

A Mission to London

BY 1896, MARCONI had reached a turning point. He knew of no technical limit to the range of his radio system but had gone as far as he could with the resources he had. To make further developments, he needed money. By this time, his father was convinced that his work was important and helped him apply to the Italian Post Office for funding. To Marconi, the advantages of using radio waves rather than wires to send messages were clear, but the Post Office didn't agree and turned the proposal down.

Annie Marconi came to her son's rescue. Her nephew, Henry Jameson-Davis, lived in London. He was an engineer with friends in the Post Office, which was responsible for the British telegraph system. After an exchange of letters,

BELOW: *Map showing places where Marconi lived and worked.*

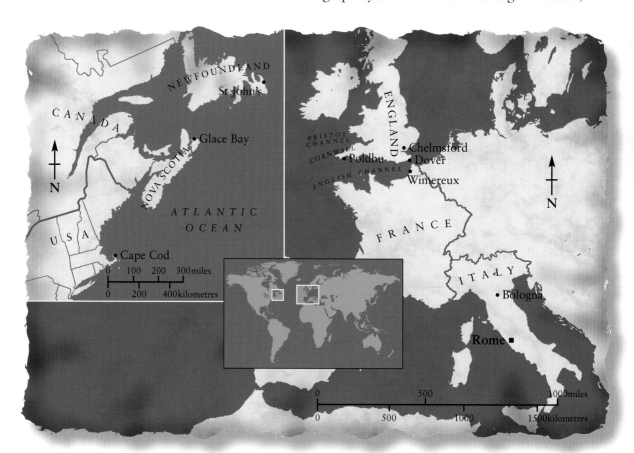

ABOVE: *The opening of the Tower Bridge, London, two years before Marconi's arrival in England. After being rejected by the Italian Post Office, Marconi was determined to make his mark in England.*

Annie and Guglielmo—still only 21—set off for England, which would be home to Marconi for many years.

Marconi's visit started badly. The customs officials were very suspicious of the mysterious wires and tubes he had brought with him and submitted the delicate apparatus to a thorough examination. He and Henry had to repair the damage done, before Marconi could start work. Once his equipment was working satisfactorily again, Marconi had two goals: to make a patent application so that his ideas could not be stolen, and to convince the British Post Office that development of his invention was worth funding.

A PARTNERSHIP

Through Jameson-Davis, Marconi was introduced to William Preece, the Chief Engineer of the Post Office. By a stroke of luck, Preece had already tried to develop radio systems to save lives at sea.

Preece invited Marconi to his house to demonstrate and explain his system. It was one of the most important moments of Marconi's life. The unknown 21-year-old inventor, lacking scientific qualifications, had to convince Preece that he had succeeded where Preece himself had failed. But Marconi was determined, intelligent, mature—and a natural showman.

RIGHT: *William Preece, Chief Engineer of the British Post Office when Marconi came to London in 1896. Preece had been one of the first telegraph engineers.*

Preece was impressed, and he agreed to demonstrate Marconi's system to his colleagues at the Post Office.

The first public demonstration of radio took place on July 27, 1896. Marconi, Preece, and a group of scientists and officials stood on the roof of the General Post Office building in London with a radio transmitter. On another building over half a mile away, a radio receiver had been set up with a simple printer attached to it. The demonstration was a complete success. When Marconi sent his test messages, they were tapped out almost instantly by the printer. The audience was amazed and impressed, particularly because there were several buildings between the transmitter and receiver.

BELOW: *Marconi in 1896, the year he went to London and made the first public demonstration of radio communication.*

THE CHALLENGE OF DISTANCE

Within a few weeks, Preece had organized another demonstration, this time spanning 4 miles (6.4 km) across Salisbury Plain. It was as successful as the first. In the audience were members of the War Office. They quickly realized that radio signaling could be a vital tool in war, when rapid communication is essential and telegraph cables are so vulnerable to sabotage.

Other demonstrations followed rapidly, and each time the distance was increased. In May 1897, Marconi showed that radio signals could be sent across the sea—an important point to prove since communication with ships was the main area in which telegraphs could not be used. This

BELOW: *Post Office engineers, checking the equipment Marconi used to detect a radio signal sent across the Bristol Channel in 1897. The seated engineer is examining the paper tape on which the messages received are printed out in Morse code.*

demonstration took place over the Bristol Channel. At first it seemed that the signals would not come through. For two days Marconi fiddled with the equipment, coaxing it to work. Then, on the third day, the messages were received over a distance of almost 9 miles (14 km).

The Businessman

By now it was clear that Marconi's system was a significant breakthrough. It was time for him to set up a company to make sure that it was a commercial success.

Marconi was an excellent businessman. He was good at organizing things, had a flair for publicity, and took great care in selecting highly skilled people to work for him. He then made sure they had the training and support they needed to do a good job. As a result, however, his relationship with Preece and with the Post Office suffered. His company was seen as a rival, and the Post Office began to set up experimental radio stations of its own.

IN THEIR OWN WORDS

"I am uncertain as to the final results of my system. My discovery was not the result of long hours of logical thought, but of experiments with machines invented by other men to which I applied certain improvements."

MARCONI IN 1897.

BELOW: *Marconi's radio works —the first radio factory in the world—in Chelmsford, England.*

SUCCESS AT HOME

The challenge of distance and possible competition in developing wireless apparatus were not Marconi's only problems in 1897. All young Italian men were required to serve in the military, and Marconi was concerned that he might be recalled to Italy at any moment. His English relatives suggested he could avoid this by becoming a British citizen, but Marconi preferred to remain Italian.

Now that Marconi's demonstrations were attracting worldwide interest, members of the Italian government were anxious that Marconi remain loyal to Italy. They decided that Marconi *should* carry out his military service—in London! They also invited him to demonstrate his radio system in Italy, which Marconi was only too happy to do. After an anxious moment when he had to find something to support the radio aerial, he transmitted the message "Viva l'Italia."

ABOVE: *Marconi (seated, fourth from right), stylishly dressed as usual, demonstrating his radio to officials of the Italian navy in 1897.*

Marconi was soon being invited to dinners given in his honor, and the press enthusiastically reported his successes, including his introduction to the King and Queen of Italy. He rapidly became a national hero.

During this time, Marconi stayed at his family home in Bologna. He had finally proved that his early experiments and interests had been anything but a waste of time, and his father treated him as an honored guest.

But there was serious work to do, too. While in Italy, Marconi made further investigations into the range of radio signals and confirmed that communication between ships and the shore was possible. When he returned to England later that year, he was ready to give even more dramatic demonstrations of the power of radio.

IN THEIR OWN WORDS

"Marconi's first demonstration for the Italian Naval Ministry came within a hair's breadth of failure. He intended to transmit a message from one floor of the building to the next, but after preparing the equipment he suddenly realized that he did not have a pole to support the aerial. After a brief moment of panic, the inventor noticed a broom, hooked it to a wire, and asked one of the people in the room to hold it in the air.... Once the equipment had been suitably arranged, Marconi sat down at the telegraph key and speedily tapped out a message, causing enthusiasm and surprise amongst everyone in attendance. On the narrow ribbon of paper connected to the Morse receiver, the words 'Viva l'Italia' were spelled out in dots and dashes."

GIANCARLO MASINI, IN HIS BOOK *MARCONI* (MARSILIO PUBLISHING, 1976).

LEFT: *A Marconi radio communication system on board a liner in the 1900s. Two Morse tappers for sending messages are on the desk at the right of the picture. The operator is writing down the message he is receiving through his headphones.*

Across the Seas

TUNING

As radio messages multiplied, a big problem emerged: all the receivers could hear all the messages from all the transmitters! Marconi solved this difficulty by tuning his systems and transmitting different signals on different radio wavelengths. This also reduced the power needed to send signals.

BY 1897, MARCONI'S demonstrations had convinced almost everyone that radio communication was a practical proposition. But in order to send signals, bulky equipment with large aerials was required. If radio was to become a commercial success, permanent transmitting stations would be needed, so the first job of Marconi's company was to set up radio stations along the south coast of Great Britain. With their huge aerials, about 100 feet (30 m) high, these stations attracted a lot of interest. Marconi's fame continued to grow.

Although radio transmissions had barely begun, in 1897 they saved lives for the first time. A new radio link between the Goodwin Sands lighthouse and Dover was used to summon a lifeboat when a ship was wrecked on the treacherous sands. At last, Marconi and Preece's dream of saving lives by radio was beginning to come true.

Soon after, radio messages were used to report the Kingstown yacht races as they happened. Even when no one could see the yachts in the mist, radio messages from on board kept listeners up to date.

Meanwhile, Marconi continued in his quest to increase the distance between transmitters. First, he sent signals across the English Channel to France—the first radio link between different countries. The obvious next goal was to send a signal across the Atlantic Ocean, demonstrating that radio could replace the longest telegraph link in existence.

LEFT: *The aerial in Wimereux, France, used for the first cross-channel radio link.*

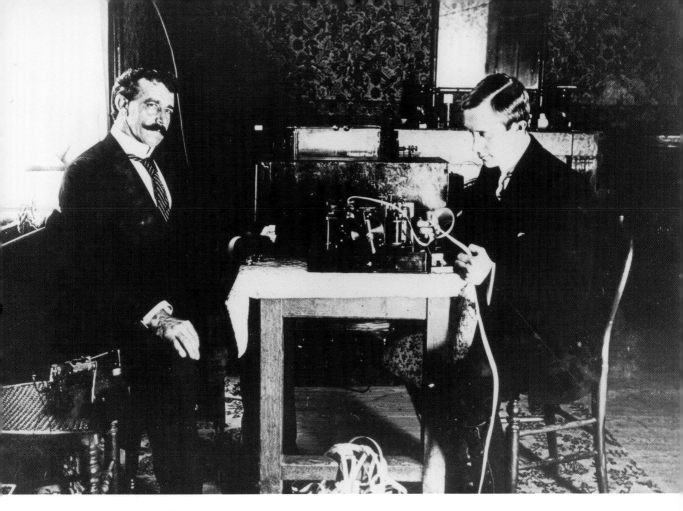

IN THEIR OWN WORDS

"If the capacity of ocean cables is not very soon increased by such electrical improvements as [Marconi] has in mind, the inventive genius of this age will be open to accusation of not keeping up with its urgent requirements. We understand that at twenty-five cents a word, the fourteen Atlantic cables now in operation are fully occupied during the business hours of the day. That means that in this matter, demand has outrun supply."

FROM *THE NEW YORK TIMES*, DECEMBER 17, 1901.

MARCONI'S DREAM

A transatlantic radio signal posed huge problems for Marconi. The distance was far greater than anything previously attempted, and the curve of the Earth might cut off all signals over such a long range; Marconi still wasn't sure how they made their way beyond the horizon.

This was the biggest project Marconi had ever attempted. He decided to set up a two-way system so that messages could be sent and received at both ends. He and his team selected suitable sites on each continent— Poldhu in Cornwall, England, and Cape Cod in the United States. Next, he supervised the construction of two vast rings of high power aerials. Each ring was 200 feet (61 m) high and 200 feet (61 m) across.

BELOW: *The aerial constructed at Poldhu, Cornwall, in preparation for the first transatlantic radio link. The aerial was blown down by a storm before it could be used.*

BELOW RIGHT: *Following the storm, a smaller aerial was constructed.*

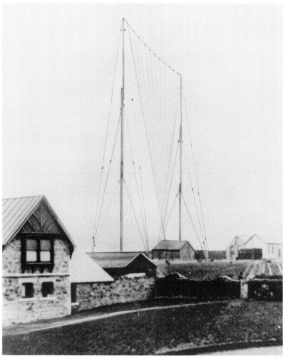

Storms and Signals

But Marconi had left the weather out of his careful plans. On September 15, 1901, a gale struck Poldhu. It tore down the ring of aerials and left behind only twisted wreckage. Just two months later the same fate struck the station at Cape Cod. For once, and only briefly, Marconi backed down a little. He contented himself with trying to send one-way signals only, from Poldhu to Canada. So although the Poldhu station needed to be repaired, in Canada just a single wire was needed, raised into the air by balloons and kites. This time, Marconi selected St. John's in Newfoundland as the receiving point and went there himself.

Again the weather nearly defeated Marconi, but after a balloon and a kite had been swept away, he finally heard the faint triple beep of the letter "S" from Poldhu. The Atlantic Ocean had been spanned by radio.

BELOW: *Across the Atlantic on the coast of Newfoundland, Marconi (far left) watches while his assistants struggle with the kite that would carry the receiving aerial.*

IN THEIR OWN WORDS

"I now felt for the first time absolutely certain that the day would come when mankind would be able to send messages without wires not only across the Atlantic but between the farthermost ends of the Earth."

MARCONI'S REACTION TO THE FIRST TRANSATLANTIC RADIO TRANSMISSION.

"Any other machine enables the inventor to shut himself up in a room and announce results when it is wise for him to do so. Wireless telegraphy is different, especially in the way that we labor. It is not a case of one machine here and one in England, but of half a machine here, and another half in England"

MARCONI IN 1903.

LOVE AND HONOR

The next year, Marconi's company announced the opening of a full commercial radio service between Poldhu and Glace Bay in Nova Scotia, Canada. The first message was sent on December 15, 1902, and a news service began on March 28, 1903. Marconi, who always liked to be in full control, was reluctant to allow the public announcements of the services before they had been thoroughly tested. As it turned out, his caution proved sensible. Only nine days later, on April 6, the Glace Bay aerial collapsed due to the weight of the ice that had formed on it.

Over the next few years, Marconi and his team patiently developed their radio systems. There was a brief interruption in 1904 when Marconi, now rich and famous, fell in love with Beatrice O'Brien, a 19-year-old Irish girl whom he met when they were both guests on a private island. They were married the following year, a year in which Marconi also started to use directional aerials that allowed signals to be aimed at the receiving station. This greatly increased their range.

RIGHT: *Marconi and his team, at the radio station at Glace Bay, Canada, in 1902.*

In 1906, Marconi and Beatrice's first daughter, Lucia, was born—but sadly she died when she was only a few weeks old. Another daughter, Degna, was born in 1908 and a third, Gioia, in 1916. Their son Giulio was born in 1910.

In 1908, the passengers of two ships that collided in the middle of the Atlantic Ocean were rescued by a radio message. A total of 1,700 lives had been saved by Marconi's astounding invention.

In 1909, Marconi received the highest honor the scientific world can give: a Nobel Prize, for his pioneering work in radio research. The only problem was that he had to share the prize with Professor Karl F. Braun, whose company was a rival to that of Marconi. The next year, radio was used for a very different reason—to signal the discovery of a murderer, Dr. Hawley H. Crippen, on board a ship to Canada.

ABOVE: *Marconi with his first wife Beatrice and their three children, Degna, Giulio, and Gioia.*

BELOW: *The arrest of Dr. Crippen and his accomplice Ethel Le Neve.*

IN THEIR OWN WORDS

"On the third day I gave my wireless operator a message for Liverpool: One hundred and thirty miles west of Lizard ...have strong suspicions that Crippen, London cellar murderer, and accomplice are among saloon passengers...."

"I remember [the disguised Dr. Crippen] sitting in a deckchair, looking at the wireless aerials and listening to the crackling of our crude spark-transmitter, and remarking to me what a wonderful invention it was."

FROM CAPTAIN KENDALL'S REPORT OF HIS DISCOVERY OF CRIPPEN, 1910.

ARRESTATION DU DOCTEUR CRIPPEN ET DE MISS LE NEVE SUR LE PONT DU «MONTROSE»

THE *TITANIC*

Marconi traveled all over the world, crossing the Atlantic more than fifty times without mishap, but his most dangerous journey was in Italy. In 1912, the car he was driving crashed into another on a mountain road. A splinter of glass was embedded in Marconi's right eye, and a few weeks later, the eye had to be removed.

Over the years, radio messages saved many shipwreck victims, but the most famous story relates to the *Titanic*, the world's largest and most luxurious ocean liner. The *Titanic* was supposed to be unsinkable. But when it struck an iceberg on April 14, 1912, it took just two hours and forty minutes for the ship to fill with water and sink, and frantic radio messages were being sent the whole time.

The Rescue

There *was* a ship close enough to have saved everyone on board before the *Titanic* sank, but there was no one operating its radio receiver at the time. Radio was still regarded by many as a novelty and was not yet installed in all ships. Instead, another ship, the *Carpathia*, heard the message over 56 miles (90 km) away and arrived two hours after the *Titanic* had sunk—in time to save some passengers, but too late for the 1,513 who perished. One of them could have been Marconi, who had planned to be on the voyage himself.

LEFT: *A painting of the "unsinkable"* Titanic *colliding with an iceberg.*

IN THEIR OWN WORDS

"Imagination is filled once more by the wonderful part played by wireless telegraphy in the story of the Titanic .... But for this new instrument of communication she might have passed from our human ken [knowledge], her fate forever unknown."

THE TIMES, APRIL 16, 1912.

ABOVE: *Survivors of the* Titanic *on board the* Carpathia.

BELOW: *A cartoon about Marconi and the* Titanic. *The caption reads "Marconi to Father Neptune—I can beat you out any time if you will only give me a few more of these lifeboats."*

The Patriot

ABOVE: *Marconi in 1914, having been made a Knight of the Grand Cross of the Royal Victorian Order. He was awarded nineteen other similar honors during his life from many countries.*

In 1914, Marconi and Beatrice were guests on the English ship H.M.S. *Leo*, one of hundreds taking part in a naval review. Afterward, the ships were preparing to return to their ports when a radio message from the British admiralty ordered that they prepare for battle. Meanwhile, German ships received their own radio instruction: They must all return to port at once. The next day, another German radio message was picked up in London. It was a declaration of war. One of the most terrible wars in history had begun.

The War Machine

Marconi returned to Rome, Italy, and was at once personally involved in the war. Radio was an important war tool, as he had always known it would be, but it was not just his technical skills that were needed. Marconi was popular the

RIGHT: *Marconi (center) on a battlefield during World War I (1914–1918).*

world over, especially in England, so he was an ideal negotiator on behalf of Italy. And he was a staunch patriot, so there was no doubt he could be trusted.

Marconi was given many tasks during the war, some of which still remain secret. He may even have been involved in discussions about whether Italy should enter the war on the side of Britain. We do know that he improved the mobile wireless stations used on the front line, he negotiated with Britain to reduce the cost of its coal to Italy, and he studied the possibilities of radio for use in aircraft. He also invented a special short-range radio system for transmitting secret messages between warships, and finally he developed a system to track the sources of enemy radio signals.

In 1918 World War I came to an end, leaving more than nine million people dead. Marconi's inventions had proven to be invaluable tools of war, and they remain so today.

FAME, FORTUNE, AND FASCISM

Elettra

After his years of hard work, Marconi decided to enjoy his enormous wealth. He had loved boats ever since his father gave him a tiny one as a child, and now he bought himself something special: a luxury yacht, which he named *Elettra*. It had a crew of thirty and was big enough to travel almost anywhere. Marconi turned it into a floating home, not only for himself but for many friends and relatives, too. It was like a tiny kingdom, with Marconi as the king who insisted that meals be served to the second!

BELOW: *Marconi's yacht, laboratory, and home,* Elettra.

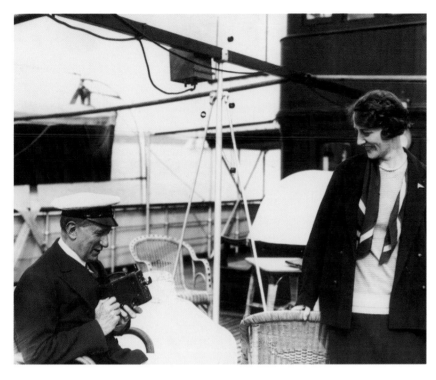

LEFT: *Marconi with his second wife Cristina, on board* Elettra.

BELOW: *Marconi (left) at the Italian Royal Academy in 1930, with the Italian Fascist dictator Benito Mussolini (center).*

Divorce

During the war—and even before—Marconi and Beatrice had been gradually drifting apart, in part because Marconi had several girlfriends over the years. Eventually, in 1924, they were divorced, and Beatrice re-married the next year. Three years later, Marconi married Cristina Bezzi-Scali, a beautiful Italian woman less than half his age. Their daughter Elettra was born in 1930.

Fascism

In 1923, Marconi joined the Italian Fascist Party, an ultra right-wing group that was later to fight in World War II alongside the Nazis. The party encouraged complete devotion to the Italian State, at the expense of many individual rights and freedoms.

Radio Days

THE FIRST REGULAR daily broadcasting service was started by the Marconi company from Chelmsford, England, in 1920. An American scientist named Reginald Fessenden had discovered how to send the human voice by radio in 1902, opening the way for entertainment broadcasting.

On Christmas Eve, 1906, Fessenden made the first ever broadcast of speech and music. It was a short violin recital and a poetry reading, and it could be received hundreds of miles away.

At the outset, the radio engineers played their own musical instruments, but the broadcasts were so popular that a few months later a famous singer named Nellie Melba broadcast a selection of songs in French, Italian, and English.

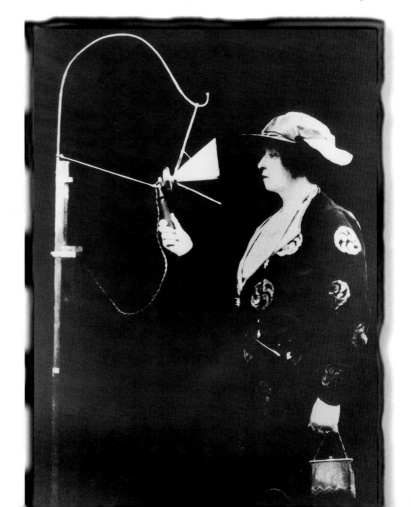

RIGHT: *Dame Nellie Melba, a famous opera singer, at the microphone in the radio studio at the Chelmsford Marconi Works in 1920.*

LEFT: *An early radio studio, with an actress at the microphone.*

BELOW: *This 1950s radio was made in the shape of an owl.*

The broadcast could be heard all over Europe and in the United States, too. The same year, the first commercial radio broadcasts in the United States began and domestic radio receivers were first produced by the American Westinghouse Company.

Early Radios

The first radios were very expensive to buy, but eager amateurs all over the world built their own receivers to tune into broadcasts from the fledgling radio stations. These early stations were difficult to establish, since there was a lot of opposition from the government. But there was also great public demand for them.

To keep people interested in buying radio receivers, all sorts of amazing designs appeared. Some radios were even gold plated, while others came equipped with mink coats!

WORLDWIDE WIRELESS

Ever since he was a child, Marconi had dreamed of a time when the whole world would be linked by radio. However, although he worked hard to set up such a system, there were many problems. The Imperial Wireless Scheme, as it was called, was something that many countries wanted to become involved in—on their own terms. Negotiation, argument, and discussion dragged on for years, and the project was severely delayed by World War I.

BELOW: *Marconi (center), supervising the positioning of an aerial aboard* Elettra *in 1930.*

But Marconi knew that there was a major technical problem, too. Radio transmitter stations would have to be enormously powerful to transmit messages that could be received over the huge distances involved.

Beam Stations

In 1923, following experiments on board *Elettra*, Marconi had the answer. By using shortwave radio signals, it was possible to send messages in a beam aimed in a particular direction. This greatly increased their range, just as a bulb can light up distant objects when it is given direction by being installed in a flashlight.

The next year, Marconi's company signed a contract with the British Government to build the first beam station, and by 1927 a worldwide network had been established with radio links between Britain, South Africa, North and South America, India, and Australia.

LEFT: *A beam station in Grimsby, England.*

"…humanity has gained a new force, a new weapon which knows no frontiers, a new method for which distance is no obstacle, a force destined to promote peace by enabling us better to fulfill what has always been essentially a human need — that of communicating with one another."

MARCONI IN 1927.

The beam stations were incredibly well designed. The shortwave transmitters were so good that forty years later when the Science Museum asked for a worn-out one, it was told there weren't any—they were all still working!

Wireless was on its way, under the name of broadcasting, and moving rapidly in a direction that Marconi had never dreamed possible in the 1890s.

LEFT: *A variety of advertisements for Marconi's worldwide radio communication system.*

SHORTWAVES

Marconi never stopped developing his radio systems. One of his fascinations was with shortwaves. He had used them in the war for short-distance communications, but little was known about them. For many years it was thought that only longwaves could travel long distances, but Marconi's experiments showed that shortwaves could be used for long-range communication, too. Shortwave radio transmitters had much smaller aerials than longwave, used less power, and were more directional.

Radar

One major use of shortwave radio is radar, a system used to detect objects at a distance by bouncing radio waves off them, which Marconi helped to invent. In 1933, he noticed

BELOW: *Marconi (left) in the radio cabin of* Elettra. *The yacht provided an ideal base for his ongoing research.*

WAVELENGTHS

The radio waves that Marconi worked with ranged in length from less than an inch to more than 12 miles (20 kms). Today's radio transmissions range from about 6 feet to about 1 1/4 miles, while television broadcasts use waves about 3 to 20 feet long. Radar uses waves from half an inch to 40 inches (1–100 cm) in length and mobile phone wavelengths are around 12 to 16 inches (30–40 cm) (see picture on right of a woman in Shanghai, China, using a mobile phone). Microwave ovens and deep-space radio communication systems both use radio waves about 5 inches (13 cm) long.

that a car passing about a mile away caused interference on his radio. He realized that the radio waves he was using were being reflected from the car.

Marconi knew this could be an important discovery and conducted secret research for the Italian government over the next few years, finding out how to detect boats and planes by bouncing shortwaves off them. This work couldn't be kept completely secret, so rumors were allowed to circulate that Marconi was developing a "death ray" that could stop cars, planes, and ships, and kill people and animals.

Marconi Therapy

In fact, Marconi developed a use of radio for healing rather than harming people. He discovered that microwaves could be used to warm the body from inside, a technique that is still used to help people with muscle and joint pain. In Italy, it is known as Marconi Therapy.

IN THEIR OWN WORDS

"Mankind is on the verge of discoveries quite as momentous as the discovery of fire. Who knows where the future will take us?"

MARCONI IN 1931.

NOTHING ON THE RADIO

All Marconi's dreams and more had come true. He was incredibly rich, famous, and popular. In 1929, the king of Italy gave him the hereditary title of "Marchese," making him a member of the Italian nobility. He had been showered with many other honors, too, but what mattered to Marconi more than anything was that his radio systems had linked the whole world and saved thousands of lives. After the success of the shortwave beam stations, Marconi took less interest in his company and began to spend more time in Italy.

Marconi had been baptized as a Catholic but had never taken religion very seriously until his second marriage. Now he agreed to install a shortwave radio station in the Vatican, so that the Pope could communicate with Catholics around the world. Two years later, he installed an experimental radio–telephone system between the Vatican and the Pope's summer home. The system used a beam of microwaves that

BELOW: *Marconi (second from left) with Pope Pius XI (second from right), during the installation of the shortwave radio in the Pope's summer residence. On the far right is Cardinal Pacelli, who later became Pope Pius XII.*

ABOVE: *Marconi, with his youngest daughter Elettra and his second wife Cristina.*

ABOVE: *A monument above Poldhu Bay, Cornwall, England, to commemorate Marconi and his first transatlantic radio link.*

made it very difficult for anyone but the users to listen in on messages.

In 1927, Marconi had a heart attack and didn't fully recover until 1930. Following an exhausting world tour, he had a more severe attack in Venice in 1934. He shrugged off his poor health but was ill again the following year—the year in which Italy attacked Abyssinia (now Ethiopia) and was criticized by England, France, and many other countries. Marconi undertook strenuous diplomatic missions in support of the Italian cause and had another heart attack the following year. From then on, he knew his time was short, and he died in Rome on July 20, 1937. He was 63 years old.

To commemorate Marconi's death, all radios around the world fell silent for two minutes. They would never be silent again.

IN THEIR OWN WORDS

"What other men had been content to prove impossible, he accomplished; and this is surely greatness. The history of wireless communication has been a history of miracles; but the true miracle…is the life of a man —the vision and the faith, the patient labor illuminated by the unshakable resolve, which surmount all the barriers and in the end confound the wise."

THE TIMES, JULY 21,1937.

The Legacy of Marconi

AFTER MARCONI'S DEATH, many of the effects he experimented with led to breakthroughs in technology. Radar has matured into a highly reliable and valuable system, and radios have become ever smaller and more efficient—and so cheap that most people can afford one.

Marconi would have been amazed that radio messages can be bounced off satellites in space. Through the use of satellites like these, small radios on ships and other vehicles can find their own position on Earth to within a few yards.

Television allows people to see all over the planet and beyond without leaving their homes, and mobile phones help millions to keep in touch. Both systems send their

ABOVE: *An example of one of the tiny portable radios available today.*

BELOW: *The world's largest radio telescope dish in Arecibo, Puerto Rico. It is used for studying the Earth's atmosphere, for astronomy, and for attempts at radio communication with extraterrestrial intelligence.*

ABOVE: *Lifeboat services now operate throughout much of the world and are still dependent on radio to alert them to boats in danger.*

signals by radio. Meanwhile, the microwaves that so fascinated Marconi in later life are now used to defrost and cook food far more quickly than conventional ovens.

Space probes have explored the whole solar system, and radio is essential both to control them and to receive images and other information from planets, moons, comets, and asteroids. Radio signals can be picked up from the farthest reaches of the universe, and radio receivers can even pick up the last fading glow of the Big Bang that started the universe more than 12 billion years ago.

IN THEIR OWN WORDS

"The day will come when every ship will carry wireless and every port will have a wireless station. . . . If my invention never accomplishes anything else than to save the passengers and crew of one ship, it will amply repay me for all the money I have spent on it."

MARCONI, INTERVIEWED IN 1902.

Timeline

1844

The first telegraph message is sent by Alexander Graham Bell from Washington, D.C., to Baltimore, Maryland.

1866

Transatlantic telegraph cable is successfully completed.

1873

James Clerk-Maxwell predicts the existence of what are now called radio waves.

1874

APRIL 25: Guglielmo Marconi is born in Bologna, Italy.

1887

Heinrich Hertz demonstrates radio.

1892

Edouard Branley invents the coherer.

1894

Marconi begins to experiment with radio.

1895

Marconi transmits radio signals across a range of more than half a mile.

1896

Marconi patents his early radio system.
Marconi and his mother go to England, and the first public trial of radio takes place in London.

1897

Marconi transmits a radio signal across the Bristol Channel, demonstrating that radio messages can be sent across water.
Marconi sets up the Wireless Telegraph and Signal Company Ltd. (later to become the Marconi Company) in Chelmsford, England.

1898

JULY: The *Daily Express* becomes the first newspaper to obtain news by wireless.
Wireless is used for the first time in naval maneuvers.

1899

Marconi sends signals across the English Channel from England to France.

1901

Marconi sends radio signal across the Atlantic Ocean from Poldhu, England, to St. John's, Canada.
Marconi and Dr. Lee De Forest compete to report the America's Cup yacht race by radio.

1902

First broadcast of human voice by Reginald Fessenden.

1903

The first regular radio broadcasts between the United States and England begin.

1905

Marconi marries Beatrice O'Brien and introduces the directional aerial.

1906

Marconi and Beatrice's first daughter, Lucia, is born and dies within a few weeks.
First broadcast of a radio program containing speech and music, by Fessenden.
JANUARY: The first radio is advertised to the public in the United States, claiming to receive signals up to one mile.
DECEMBER: Fessenden becomes the first person to broadcast a program of speech and music.

1908

Degna Marconi is born.

1910

Marconi and Beatrice's son, Giulio, is born.

1912

APRIL 14: The *Titanic* sinks, and the survivors are saved by a wireless message.
Marconi loses an eye, as a result of a car crash in Italy.

1909

Marconi wins the Nobel Prize, which he receives jointly with Karl Ferdinand Braun.

1914

World War I begins.
Marconi begins shortwave radio experiments.

1916

Gioia Marconi is born.

1918

World War I ends.
First regular daily broadcasting service started by Marconi company.
First regular broadcasts begin in the United States.
A radio message from the Marconi longwave station at Caernarvon, in Wales, is received in Australia over a distance of nearly 11,000 miles (18,000 km).

1919

Marconi is sent as an Italian delegate to the Peace Conference in Paris, where he signs treaties with Austria and Belgium.

1920

First regular daily broadcasting service is started by Marconi Company from Chelmsford, England.

1923

Marconi joins the Italian Fascist Party.

1924

Marconi and Beatrice divorce.
Marconi Company signs contract with the British Government to build the first Beam Station.

1926–1927

Britain–Canada beam service opened.
Beam services link Britain to Australia, India, South America, and South Africa. First car radios introduced.

1927

Marconi marries Cristina Bezzi-Scali.

1930

Cristina and Marconi have a daughter, Elettra.

1931

Marconi installs a shortwave radio station in the Vatican in Rome.

1937

JULY 20: Marconi dies.

1957

First satellite, *Sputnik 1*, sends radio signals to Earth.

1962

First communication satellite, *Telstar*, launched.

Glossary

Aerial
Metal plate, wire, or rod used to transmit or receive radio waves.

Atmosphere
The layer of gases surrounding the Earth or any other planet or star.

Broadcast
To send a radio signal over a wide area.

Cable
An insulated electrical conductor.

Coherer
Instrument used in the early 20th century to detect radio waves. When radio waves are present, the metallic particles in the coherer stick together and conduct electricity.

Fascist
Extreme right-wing political group.

Ionosphere
A layer in the atmosphere that contains electrically charged particles produced by the effect of X rays and ultraviolet light from the sun. It reflects some radio waves.

Loudspeaker
Device that converts electrical signals into sound.

Microwaves
Electromagnetic waves with wavelengths between about a fraction of an inch to 12 inches (1 mm–30 cm).

Modify
To change.

Nazis
Members of the National Socialist Party, an extreme right-wing political group.

Nobel Prize
An annual award for outstanding achievement in physics, chemistry, literature, international peace, or economics.

Patent
Official document that registers an idea as someone's property. Other people may not use it without permission from the owner of the patent.

Radar
Radio Detection and Ranging. A method of detecting distant objects by bouncing radiowaves off them and analyzing the echoes received.

Range
The maximum distance over which a signal can be received.

Receiver
An instrument that can pick up radio signals.

Satellite
Object in orbit around a planet or moon. Since 1957, thousands of artificial satellites have been put into orbit around the Earth for communications, weather forecasting, and scientific and military purposes.

Shortwaves
Radio waves with wavelengths of less than about 100 yards.

Signals
An electrical or radio impulse either transmitted or received.

Spark-gap receiver
An early type of radio receiver that produced a tiny electrical spark when it received a radio signal.

Static
Electromagnetic interference to radio signals, which can be heard as crackling or hissing.

Telegraph
Communications system in which pulses of electricity are sent down wires.

Transatlantic
Across the Atlantic Ocean.

Transmitter
Instrument that sends out electrical or radio signals.

Further Information

BOOKS FOR YOUNGER READERS

Birch, Beverley. *Guglielmo Marconi: Radio Pioneer (Giants of Science).* Woodbridge, CT: Blackbirch Marketing, 2001.

Birch, Beverley. *Marconi's Battle for Radio (Science Stories Series).* Hauppage NY: Barrons Juveniles, 1996.

Parker, Steve. *Guglielmo Marconi and Radio (Science Discoveries).* Broomall PA: Chelsea House Publishers, 1995.

FOR OLDER READERS

Marconi, Degna. *My Father, Marconi.* Tonawanda, NY: Guernica Editions Inc., 2002.

Marconi, Maria Cristina, *Marconi My Beloved.* Brookline Village, MA: Dante University of America Press Inc., 1999.

WEBSITES

http://www.fgm.it/
The Italian website of the Guglielmo Marconi Foundation, with extensive information about Marconi and his work. In Italian and English.

http://www.marconiusa.org/index.html
Website of the United States Marconi Museum with a detailed account of the role radio played in rescuing survivors of the *Titanic* disaster.

http://www.nobel.se/
The official site of the Nobel Foundation. Use the search tool to find out about Guglielmo Marconi and other Nobel prize-winners.

Index

Numbers in **bold** are pages where there is a photograph or an illustration.